THE

9%

EDGE

Planner

"The whole point of starting a business is to build a machine that generates revenue and creates wealth, so you can stop trading time for money."

— **Candy Valentino**

CANDY VALENTINO

YOUR BEST QUARTER YET

THE 9% EDGE *Planner*

A QUARTERLY GUIDE TO HELP YOU MAINTAIN CLARITY, STAY FOCUSED, AND KEEP YOU ON TRACK FOR SUCCESS

WILEY

Published by John Wiley & Sons, Inc., Hoboken, New Jersey.
Published simultaneously in Canada.

For general information on our other products and services or for technical support, please contact our Customer Care Department within the United States at (800) 762-2974, outside the United States at (317) 572-3993 or fax (317) 572-4002.

Wiley also publishes its books in a variety of electronic formats. Some content that appears in print may not be available in electronic formats. For more information about Wiley products, visit our web site at www.wiley.com.

Library of Congress Cataloging-in-Publication Data is Available:
ISBN 9781394309535 (Paperback)
ISBN 9781394309542 (ePub)
ISBN 9781394309559 (ePDF)

Cover Design: Wiley
Cover Image: © phochi/Getty Images

SKY10089723_103124

WELCOME TO THE NEXT QUARTER OF YOUR WEALTHIEST YEAR YET

Dear Entrepreneur,

Welcome to the next quarter of your most successful and wealthiest year yet!

I'm thrilled to introduce you to *The 9% Edge Quarterly Planner*, meticulously designed to elevate your business to new heights of revenue, profits, and growth. This planner isn't a book to read. It's a tool based on science and research, drawn not only from two and a half decades of my own business experience but also from data and insights gathered from studying 2,000 businesses and 17,000 entrepreneurs.

You hold in your hands a roadmap to growth crafted from proven principles and research-backed methodologies. What's inside will give you the edge in business, as its pages are filled with strategies that separate the successful 9% from the 91% who fail within their first decade in business.

As you embark on this journey with *The 9% Edge Quarterly Planner*, remember that ideas won't change your business, your results, or your life — it's the implementation and execution of ideas that will.

Each section is designed to guide you through critical steps, and by leveraging this powerful tool you are ensuring that every goal and aspiration you have transforms from dreams into results.

If you want to maximize your results, commit to diving in daily and use this powerful tool to strategize, prioritize, and execute with precision. Make this quarter a testament to your dedication, commitment, and vision.

Let *The 9% Edge Quarterly Planner* be your companion in making new decisions, which will create new behaviors, which will build new habits, which will give you new results — in every area of life.

Thank you for choosing to embark on this journey. Together, we will navigate challenges, seize new opportunities, and **make this quarter not just successful, but the beginning of your wealthiest year yet.**

To your success,

Candy
VALENTINO

The 9% Edge Quarterly Planner Methodology

When you follow the 9% Edge Quarterly Planner Methodology, you will reverse engineer your desired goals and break them down into actionable, measurable steps. Each section allows you to use data to prioritize which actions will move the needle forward and which are draining your productivity and ultimately your results.

QUARTERLY GOAL
What is your goal for this next quarter? Which Business Metrics do you need to focus on for the next quarter to achieve that goal?

Our approach is rooted in precision and strategic alignment. Each quarter begins with an assessment of where your business stands and where it aims to go. We set clear, measurable objectives and leverage metrics and KPIs in this process. This structure ensures that every quarter is a key step towards significant revenue growth, increased profitability, leading the business forward, and achieving your most successful and wealthiest year yet.

MONTHLY KPIS
What monthly targets do we need to hit in order to attain your Quarterly Goal? What do we need to measure so can we increase revenue or profit?

Our commitment to driving improvement continues through monthly goals. Each month, we break down quarterly objectives into actionable steps. By focusing on short-term milestones that contribute to long-term success, we keep accountability and momentum going. We monitor monthly performance to understand what's working and where adjustments are needed. Through data and analytics, we ensure each month is optimized for sustainable growth and lasting profitability.

WEEKLY PLAN
What tasks and ideas will keep you on track to achieving your goals? What can you delegate, eliminate, and automate?

Each week, we do a brain dump to capture and collect any ideas or tasks that are on your mind to clear your focus for what's most important. We categorize those ideas and tasks into larger chunks, and complete the DEA exercise to determine which actions are necessary and productive, and which are preventing you from getting closer to your goals.

DAILY PLAN
What is your prioritized task list? What will help you stay focused and on track so we can compound efforts and achieve your quarterly goals?

Using the Daily Plan allows you to prioritize your tasks and maintain your health as an entrepreneur. In order to build a better business, we need to build a better entrepreneur. This will help you Prepare and Plan™ your day and to get in alignment with your goals. We even take a few moments in the evening to capture your wins and takeaways for tomorrow.

ADDITIONAL 9% EDGE RESOURCES

The only way to learn anything new is to start doing it. It takes time to develop confidence but you deserve this. Scan the QR code and discover additional 9% Edge Resources that are available for you.

- Want to make more revenue for your business and create more freedom for yourself? Read *The 9% Edge*, available anywhere books are sold.
- Want to hit the financial easy button? Check out how ProfitNow can help you and your team stay on top of your sales and systems at: **www.ProfitNow.io**
- Want free strategies and tips on continuing to make this your wealthiest year yet? Subscribe and receive weekly episodes at: **www.TheCandyValentinoShow.com**

QUARTERLY GOAL SETTING

Step 1. Determine your goal.

What is your goal for the next quarter? _____

What goal should you focus on for the next quarter?

- [ ] Revenue / Sales
- [ ] Profitability
- [ ] Buyer / Purchase Frequency
- [ ] Average Order Value

- [ ] Customer Acquisition
- [ ] Customer Conversion
- [ ] Customer Churn Rate
- [ ] Customer Lifetime Value

- [ ] Cash Flow
- [ ] Burn Rate
- [ ] Net Profit
- [ ] Retention Rate

Use that metric to write your goal.

I will increase my _____ from _____ to _____

Step 2. Determine why this goal is important to you. And why now?

Why is this goal important? _____

_____

_____

Why is this goal important now? _____

_____

_____

What will it give you? _____

_____

_____

What will it cost you if you don't do it? _____

_____

_____

What will it give you when you have achieved it? _____

_____

_____

QUARTERLY GOAL SETTING

MM _____ DD _____ YR _____ QQ _____

_____

Step 3. Brainstorm how you can achieve this goal.

What strategy could you deploy to achieve this goal? _____

_____

_____

Who might you ask for help? _____

_____

_____

How would you mitigate the constraints? _____

_____

_____

What's not working that you need to let go of? _____

_____

_____

What's already working that you might double down on? _____

_____

_____

How to Calculate Your Business Metrics

Buyer Frequency/Purchase Frequency

$$\frac{\text{Number of Orders (365 Days)}}{\text{Number of Unique Customers (365 Days)}} = \text{Purchase Frequency (PV)}$$

$$\frac{\boxed{}}{\boxed{}} = \boxed{} \text{ Your Purchase Frequency (PV)}$$

Average Order Value

$$\frac{\text{Total Revenue}}{\text{Total Number of Orders}} = \text{Average Order Value (AOV)}$$

$$\frac{\boxed{}}{\boxed{}} = \boxed{} \text{ Your Average Order Value (AOV)}$$

MONTH

1

*"IF YOU ARE NOT INTENTIONALLY BUILDING A **BUSINESS**, YOU WILL ACCIDENTALLY BUILD YOURSELF A **JOB**."*

— **Candy Valentino**

MONTH 1

Step 1. Perform the monthly goal review.

Refer back to your last month's goal. Analyze your progress below:

KPI	Target	Actual Result	Difference

What were your wins this month? _____

_____

_____

What gave you the most trouble this month? _____

_____

_____

What do you want to improve for next month? _____

_____

Step 2. Set next month's goal.

Refer back to your Quarterly Goal. Rewrite it below:

I will increase my _____ from _____ to _____

_____

What three KPIs would best track that goal?

KPI	Current Result	Target Result	Who Is Responsible

STATE OF THE UNION MEETING

The State of the Union Meeting is the best way to master your finances and radically change your business. During this two-hour meeting, you simply review the numbers from the prior month. For example, if today is November 8, you'll review October 1–31.

To learn more about the State of the Union Meeting, go to Chapter 7 of *The 9% Edge* and/or *The Candy Valentino Show*, available wherever you listen to podcasts.

Step 1. Prepare for your State of the Union Meeting.

- [ ] **Prepare (or have your bookkeeper prepare) the required business financial documents.**
  - [ ] These three critical business statements with three time periods each, for a total of nine:
    - [ ] **Financial Reports:** Income Statement, Cash Flow Statement, Balance Sheet
    - [ ] **Time Periods:** Monthly, Quarter to Date Comparison, Year to Date Comparison
  - [ ] Business Bank Statements for the month
  - [ ] Current Bank Reconciliations for the month
  - [ ] Business Software Reports
- [ ] **Block out two hours with a change of environment. You want to be in a different location from your normal working hours, where you are comfortable and productive.**

Step 2. Execute your State of the Union Meeting.

- [ ] **Determine if you need to hold meeting minutes based on your state and business structure. If so, take notes on your findings from this meeting.**
- [ ] **Analyze your documents.**
- [ ] **Use Financial Ratios to measure the data.**
- [ ] **Ask yourself the following questions:**
  - [ ] **People:** Do you need to establish performance reviews with any of your team members?
  - [ ] **Profit:** Do you need to run a profit optimization on your expenses?
  - [ ] **Process:** Do you need to create a process or system around any repetitive task?

Step 3. Determine why this goal is important to you. And why now?

Based on your State of the Union Meeting, do you need to revise your KPIs for the coming month? If so, how? _____

_____

- [ ] Delegate and calendar necessary actions.

MONTH 1

Expense Optimization

Trim the fat on your expenses to immediately impact your bottom line, find clarity, and increase stability!

Step 1. Reduce nonessential expenses.

What expenses are truly essential and which are nonessential costs?

_____

☐ Reduce nonessential expenses to immediately increase profitability.

Step 2. Renegotiate vendor contracts.

Which vendor contract terms would you like to improve? How so?

_____

How will you meet that outcome?

☐ Renegotiate terms.

☐ Shop out competitive bids.

☐ Consolidate and combine suppliers to receive bulk or volume discounts.

☐ Renegotiate vendor contracts to significantly reduce expenses.

Step 3. Review overhead expenses.

Which overhead expenses could you reduce? (utilities, office supplies, rent, insurance, etc.)

_____

☐ Renegotiate overhead expenses to save thousands over time.

Step 4. Reevaluate subscriptions and software charges.

Which subscriptions and softwares are costing you? (cloud storage, website hosting, cybersecurity, etc.)

_____

☐ Reevaluate subscriptions and software charges by eliminating what's possible and exploring options for what's necessary.

WEEK 1

Step 1. Capture and Collect any task or idea that's on your mind.

Simply transfer these items out of your head and onto the page. This is especially important as you consider your Monthly Goals. What do you need to do this week to be successful?

CAPTURE   **&**   COLLECT

"If you learn to fall in love with the process, success is no longer a destination, it becomes a way of life."

— Candy Valentino

WEEK 1

Step 2. Categorize your tasks or ideas.

Group like tasks or ideas together to create easier visualization and execution.

CATEGORIZE

Category:

_____

_____

_____

_____

_____

_____

Category:

_____

_____

_____

_____

_____

_____

Category:

_____

_____

_____

_____

_____

_____

Category:

_____

_____

_____

_____

_____

_____

Category:

_____

_____

_____

_____

_____

_____

Category:

_____

_____

_____

_____

_____

_____

Step 3. DEA: Delegate, Eliminate, and Automate.

- **Delegate:** Delegate any item possible to your team.
- **Eliminate:** Strikethrough any item that doesn't meet Pareto's Principle: 20% of your action creates 80% of your results.
- **Automate:** Write an "A" next to any items that you can use a system to automate.

DAILY SECTION

PREPARE & PLAN™ (AM)

Five Things I'm Grateful for Today...

1. _____
2. _____
3. _____
4. _____
5. _____

☐ **3x3**

How I want to **show up** today in one word:
_____

How I want to **feel** today in one word:
_____

If I only **got one thing done today,** it must be:
_____

5 AM	
6 AM	
7 AM	
8 AM	
9 AM	
10 AM	
11 AM	
12 PM	
1 PM	
2 PM	
3 PM	
4 PM	
5 PM	
6 PM	
7 PM	
8 PM	
9 PM	

DAILY SECTION

REFLECT & RESET™ (PM)

💧 I drank _____ ounces of water.   🏋 I moved my body for _____ minutes.

Something I realized or a lesson I learned today: _____
_____

Something that happened today that I really appreciated: _____
_____

☐ Shut off all electronics 30 minutes before bed.

Accomplishments:

_____
_____
_____
_____
_____

Plans for Tomorrow:

_____
_____
_____
_____
_____

Notes

_____
_____

DAILY SECTION

PREPARE & PLAN™ (AM)

Five Things I'm Grateful for Today...

1. _____
2. _____
3. _____
4. _____
5. _____

☐ **3x3**

How I want to **show up** today in one word:

_____

How I want to **feel** today in one word:

_____

If I only **got one thing done today,** it must be:

_____

5 AM
6 AM
7 AM
8 AM
9 AM
10 AM
11 AM
12 PM
1 PM
2 PM
3 PM
4 PM
5 PM
6 PM
7 PM
8 PM
9 PM

DAILY SECTION

REFLECT & RESET™ (PM)

💧 I drank _____ ounces of water.   🏋 I moved my body for _____ minutes.

Something I realized or a lesson I learned today: _____
_____

Something that happened today that I really appreciated: _____
_____

☐ Shut off all electronics 30 minutes before bed.

Accomplishments:

_____
_____
_____
_____
_____

Plans for Tomorrow:

_____
_____
_____
_____
_____

Notes

_____
_____

DAILY SECTION

MM _____ DD _____ YR _____ QQ _____

PREPARE & PLAN™ (AM)

Five Things I'm Grateful for Today...

1. _____
2. _____
3. _____
4. _____
5. _____

☐ **3x3**

How I want to **show up** today in one word:
_____

How I want to **feel** today in one word:
_____

If I only **got one thing done today,** it must be:
_____

5 AM	
6 AM	
7 AM	
8 AM	
9 AM	
10 AM	
11 AM	
12 PM	
1 PM	
2 PM	
3 PM	
4 PM	
5 PM	
6 PM	
7 PM	
8 PM	
9 PM	

DAILY SECTION

_____

REFLECT & RESET™ (PM)

🌢 I drank _____ ounces of water.   🏋 I moved my body for _____ minutes.

Something I realized or a lesson I learned today: _____

_____

Something that happened today that I really appreciated: _____

_____

☐ Shut off all electronics 30 minutes before bed.

Accomplishments:

_____
_____
_____
_____
_____

Plans for Tomorrow:

_____
_____
_____
_____
_____

Notes

_____
_____

DAILY SECTION

PREPARE & PLAN™ (AM)

Five Things I'm Grateful for Today...

1. _____
2. _____
3. _____
4. _____
5. _____

☐ **3x3**

How I want to **show up** today in one word:
_____

How I want to **feel** today in one word:
_____

If I only **got one thing done today,** it must be:
_____

| 5 AM |
| 6 AM |
| 7 AM |
| 8 AM |
| 9 AM |
| 10 AM |
| 11 AM |
| 12 PM |
| 1 PM |
| 2 PM |
| 3 PM |
| 4 PM |
| 5 PM |
| 6 PM |
| 7 PM |
| 8 PM |
| 9 PM |

DAILY SECTION

REFLECT & RESET™ (PM)

💧 I drank _____ ounces of water.   🏋 I moved my body for _____ minutes.

Something I realized or a lesson I learned today: _____

_____

Something that happened today that I really appreciated: _____

_____

☐ Shut off all electronics 30 minutes before bed.

Accomplishments:

_____
_____
_____
_____
_____

Plans for Tomorrow:

_____
_____
_____
_____
_____

Notes

_____
_____

DAILY SECTION

PREPARE & PLAN™ (AM)

Five Things I'm Grateful for Today...

1. _____
2. _____
3. _____
4. _____
5. _____

☐ **3x3**

How I want to **show up** today in one word:
_____

How I want to **feel** today in one word:
_____

If I only **got one thing done today,** it must be:
_____

5 AM	
6 AM	
7 AM	
8 AM	
9 AM	
10 AM	
11 AM	
12 PM	
1 PM	
2 PM	
3 PM	
4 PM	
5 PM	
6 PM	
7 PM	
8 PM	
9 PM	

DAILY SECTION

REFLECT & RESET™ (PM)

I drank _____ ounces of water.   I moved my body for _____ minutes.

Something I realized or a lesson I learned today: _____

_____

Something that happened today that I really appreciated: _____

_____

[ ] Shut off all electronics 30 minutes before bed.

Accomplishments:

_____

_____

_____

_____

_____

Plans for Tomorrow:

_____

_____

_____

_____

Notes

_____

_____

WEEK 2

Step 1. Capture and Collect any task or idea that's on your mind.

Simply transfer these items out of your head and onto the page. This is especially important as you consider your Monthly Goals and KPIs. What do you need to do this week to be successful?

CAPTURE & COLLECT

"Your greatest expansion will come from refinement and elimination."

— Candy Valentino

WEEK 2

Step 2. Categorize your tasks or ideas.

Group like tasks or ideas together to create easier visualization and execution.

CATEGORIZE

Category:
_____
_____
_____
_____
_____
_____

Category:
_____
_____
_____
_____
_____
_____

Category:
_____
_____
_____
_____
_____
_____

Category:
_____
_____
_____
_____
_____
_____

Category:
_____
_____
_____
_____
_____
_____

Category:
_____
_____
_____
_____
_____
_____

Step 3. DEA: Delegate, Eliminate, and Automate.

- **Delegate:** Delegate any item possible to your team.
- **Eliminate:** Strikethrough any item that doesn't meet Pareto's Principle: 20% of your action creates 80% of your results.
- **Automate:** Write an "A" next to any items that you can use a system to automate.

DAILY SECTION

PREPARE & PLAN™ (AM)

Five Things I'm Grateful for Today...

1. _____
2. _____
3. _____
4. _____
5. _____

☐ **3x3**

How I want to **show up** today in one word:

_____

How I want to **feel** today in one word:

_____

If I only **got one thing done today,** it must be:

_____

5 AM	
6 AM	
7 AM	
8 AM	
9 AM	
10 AM	
11 AM	
12 PM	
1 PM	
2 PM	
3 PM	
4 PM	
5 PM	
6 PM	
7 PM	
8 PM	
9 PM	

DAILY SECTION

REFLECT & RESET™ (PM)

💧 I drank _____ ounces of water.   🏋 I moved my body for _____ minutes.

Something I realized or a lesson I learned today: _____
_____

Something that happened today that I really appreciated: _____
_____

☐ Shut off all electronics 30 minutes before bed.

Accomplishments:

_____
_____
_____
_____
_____

Plans for Tomorrow:

_____
_____
_____
_____
_____

Notes

_____
_____

DAILY SECTION

PREPARE & PLAN™ (AM)

Five Things I'm Grateful for Today...

1. _____
2. _____
3. _____
4. _____
5. _____

☐ **3x3**

How I want to **show up** today in one word:
_____

How I want to **feel** today in one word:
_____

If I only **got one thing done today,** it must be:
_____

5 AM	
6 AM	
7 AM	
8 AM	
9 AM	
10 AM	
11 AM	
12 PM	
1 PM	
2 PM	
3 PM	
4 PM	
5 PM	
6 PM	
7 PM	
8 PM	
9 PM	

DAILY SECTION

REFLECT & RESET™ (PM)

I drank _____ ounces of water.   I moved my body for _____ minutes.

Something I realized or a lesson I learned today: _____

_____

Something that happened today that I really appreciated: _____

_____

☐ Shut off all electronics 30 minutes before bed.

Accomplishments:

_____

_____

_____

_____

_____

Plans for Tomorrow:

_____

_____

_____

_____

_____

Notes

_____

_____

DAILY SECTION

PREPARE & PLAN™ (AM)

Five Things I'm Grateful for Today...

1. _____
2. _____
3. _____
4. _____
5. _____

☐ **3x3**

How I want to **show up** today in one word:
_____

How I want to **feel** today in one word:
_____

If I only **got one thing done today,** it must be:
_____

5 AM	
6 AM	
7 AM	
8 AM	
9 AM	
10 AM	
11 AM	
12 PM	
1 PM	
2 PM	
3 PM	
4 PM	
5 PM	
6 PM	
7 PM	
8 PM	
9 PM	

DAILY SECTION

REFLECT & RESET™ (PM)

I drank _____ ounces of water.   I moved my body for _____ minutes.

Something I realized or a lesson I learned today: _____
_____

Something that happened today that I really appreciated: _____
_____

☐ Shut off all electronics 30 minutes before bed.

Accomplishments:

_____
_____
_____
_____
_____

Plans for Tomorrow:

_____
_____
_____
_____
_____

Notes

_____
_____

DAILY SECTION

PREPARE & PLAN™ (AM)

Five Things I'm Grateful for Today...

1. _____
2. _____
3. _____
4. _____
5. _____

☐ **3x3**

How I want to **show up** today in one word:
_____

How I want to **feel** today in one word:
_____

If I only **got one thing done today,** it must be:
_____

5 AM	
6 AM	
7 AM	
8 AM	
9 AM	
10 AM	
11 AM	
12 PM	
1 PM	
2 PM	
3 PM	
4 PM	
5 PM	
6 PM	
7 PM	
8 PM	
9 PM	

DAILY SECTION

REFLECT & RESET™ (PM)

💧 I drank ——————— ounces of water.   🏋 I moved my body for ——————— minutes.

Something I realized or a lesson I learned today: ————————————————————
——

Something that happened today that I really appreciated: ———————————————
——

☐ Shut off all electronics 30 minutes before bed.

Accomplishments:

——————————————————————————————————————
——————————————————————————————————————
——————————————————————————————————————
——————————————————————————————————————
——————————————————————————————————————

Plans for Tomorrow:

——————————————————————————————————————
——————————————————————————————————————
——————————————————————————————————————
——————————————————————————————————————
——————————————————————————————————————

Notes

——————————————————————————————————————
——————————————————————————————————————

DAILY SECTION

PREPARE & PLAN™ (AM)

Five Things I'm Grateful for Today...

1. _____
2. _____
3. _____
4. _____
5. _____

☐ **3x3**

How I want to **show up** today in one word:
_____

How I want to **feel** today in one word:
_____

If I only **got one thing done today,** it must be:
_____

5 AM	
6 AM	
7 AM	
8 AM	
9 AM	
10 AM	
11 AM	
12 PM	
1 PM	
2 PM	
3 PM	
4 PM	
5 PM	
6 PM	
7 PM	
8 PM	
9 PM	

DAILY SECTION

REFLECT & RESET™ (PM)

💧 I drank _____ ounces of water.   🏋 I moved my body for _____ minutes.

Something I realized or a lesson I learned today: _____

_____

Something that happened today that I really appreciated: _____

_____

☐ Shut off all electronics 30 minutes before bed.

Accomplishments:

_____

_____

_____

_____

Plans for Tomorrow:

_____

_____

_____

_____

_____

Notes

_____

_____

WEEK 3

MM _____ DD _____ YR _____ QQ _____

Step 1. Capture and Collect any task or idea that's on your mind.

Simply transfer these items out of your head and onto the page. This is especially important as you consider your Monthly Goals and KPIs. What do you need to do this week to be successful?

CAPTURE	&	COLLECT

"It will always cost you more to acquire a new customer than it will to get an existing one to buy more from you."

— Candy Valentino

WEEK 3

MM _____ DD _____ YR _____ QQ _____

Step 2. Categorize your tasks or ideas.

Group like tasks or ideas together to create easier visualization and execution.

CATEGORIZE

Category:
_____
_____
_____
_____
_____
_____

Category:
_____
_____
_____
_____
_____
_____

Category:
_____
_____
_____
_____
_____
_____

Category:
_____
_____
_____
_____
_____
_____

Category:
_____
_____
_____
_____
_____
_____

Category:
_____
_____
_____
_____
_____
_____

Step 3. DEA: Delegate, Eliminate, and Automate.

- **Delegate:** Delegate any item possible to your team.
- **Eliminate:** Strikethrough any item that doesn't meet Pareto's Principle: 20% of your action creates 80% of your results.
- **Automate:** Write an "A" next to any items that you can use a system to automate.

DAILY SECTION

PREPARE & PLAN™ (AM)

Five Things I'm Grateful for Today...

1. _____
2. _____
3. _____
4. _____
5. _____

☐ 3x3

How I want to **show up** today in one word:
_____

How I want to **feel** today in one word:
_____

If I only **got one thing done today,** it must be:
_____

5 AM	
6 AM	
7 AM	
8 AM	
9 AM	
10 AM	
11 AM	
12 PM	
1 PM	
2 PM	
3 PM	
4 PM	
5 PM	
6 PM	
7 PM	
8 PM	
9 PM	

DAILY SECTION

REFLECT & RESET™ (PM)

I drank _____ ounces of water. I moved my body for _____ minutes.

Something I realized or a lesson I learned today: _____
_____

Something that happened today that I really appreciated: _____
_____

☐ Shut off all electronics 30 minutes before bed.

Accomplishments:

_____
_____
_____
_____
_____

Plans for Tomorrow:

_____
_____
_____
_____

Notes

_____
_____

DAILY SECTION

PREPARE & PLAN™ (AM)

Five Things I'm Grateful for Today...

1. _____
2. _____
3. _____
4. _____
5. _____

☐ **3x3**

How I want to **show up** today in one word:
_____

How I want to **feel** today in one word:
_____

If I only **got one thing done today,** it must be:
_____

5 AM
6 AM
7 AM
8 AM
9 AM
10 AM
11 AM
12 PM
1 PM
2 PM
3 PM
4 PM
5 PM
6 PM
7 PM
8 PM
9 PM

DAILY SECTION

REFLECT & RESET™ (PM)

I drank _____ ounces of water.   I moved my body for _____ minutes.

Something I realized or a lesson I learned today: _____

_____

Something that happened today that I really appreciated: _____

_____

☐ Shut off all electronics 30 minutes before bed.

Accomplishments:

_____

_____

_____

_____

_____

Plans for Tomorrow:

_____

_____

_____

_____

Notes

_____

_____

DAILY SECTION

PREPARE & PLAN™ (AM)

Five Things I'm Grateful for Today...

1. _____
2. _____
3. _____
4. _____
5. _____

☐ 3x3

How I want to **show up** today in one word:
_____

How I want to **feel** today in one word:
_____

If I only **got one thing done today,** it must be:
_____

5 AM
6 AM
7 AM
8 AM
9 AM
10 AM
11 AM
12 PM
1 PM
2 PM
3 PM
4 PM
5 PM
6 PM
7 PM
8 PM
9 PM

DAILY SECTION

REFLECT & RESET™ (PM)

💧 I drank _____ ounces of water.   🏋 I moved my body for _____ minutes.

Something I realized or a lesson I learned today: _____

_____

Something that happened today that I really appreciated: _____

_____

☐ Shut off all electronics 30 minutes before bed.

Accomplishments:

_____
_____
_____
_____
_____

Plans for Tomorrow:

_____
_____
_____
_____
_____

Notes

_____
_____

DAILY SECTION

PREPARE & PLAN™ (AM)

Five Things I'm Grateful for Today...

1. _____
2. _____
3. _____
4. _____
5. _____

☐ **3x3**

How I want to **show up** today in one word:
_____

How I want to **feel** today in one word:
_____

If I only **got one thing done today,** it must be:
_____

5 AM	
6 AM	
7 AM	
8 AM	
9 AM	
10 AM	
11 AM	
12 PM	
1 PM	
2 PM	
3 PM	
4 PM	
5 PM	
6 PM	
7 PM	
8 PM	
9 PM	

DAILY SECTION

REFLECT & RESET™ (PM)

💧 I drank _____ ounces of water.   🏋 I moved my body for _____ minutes.

Something I realized or a lesson I learned today: _____
_____

Something that happened today that I really appreciated: _____
_____

☐ Shut off all electronics 30 minutes before bed.

Accomplishments:

_____
_____
_____
_____
_____

Plans for Tomorrow:

_____
_____
_____
_____
_____

Notes

_____
_____

DAILY SECTION

PREPARE & PLAN™ (AM)

Five Things I'm Grateful for Today...

1. _____
2. _____
3. _____
4. _____
5. _____

☐ **3x3**

How I want to **show up** today in one word:

_____

How I want to **feel** today in one word:

_____

If I only **got one thing done today,** it must be:

_____

5 AM
6 AM
7 AM
8 AM
9 AM
10 AM
11 AM
12 PM
1 PM
2 PM
3 PM
4 PM
5 PM
6 PM
7 PM
8 PM
9 PM

DAILY SECTION

MM _____ DD _____ YR _____ QQ _____

_____

REFLECT & RESET™ (PM)

I drank _____ ounces of water.   I moved my body for _____ minutes.

Something I realized or a lesson I learned today: _____

_____

Something that happened today that I really appreciated: _____

_____

☐ Shut off all electronics 30 minutes before bed.

Accomplishments:

_____
_____
_____
_____
_____

Plans for Tomorrow:

_____
_____
_____
_____
_____

Notes

_____
_____

WEEK 4

MM _____ DD _____ YR _____ QQ _____

Step 1. Capture and Collect any task or idea that's on your mind.

Simply transfer these items out of your head and onto the page. This is especially important as you consider your Monthly Goals and KPIs. What do you need to do this week to be successful?

CAPTURE & COLLECT

"Only what gets measured has the potential to be improved."

— Candy Valentino

WEEK 4

Step 2. Categorize your tasks or ideas.

Group like tasks or ideas together to create easier visualization and execution.

CATEGORIZE

Category:	Category:	Category:
_____	_____	_____
_____	_____	_____
_____	_____	_____
_____	_____	_____
_____	_____	_____
_____	_____	_____

Category:	Category:	Category:
_____	_____	_____
_____	_____	_____
_____	_____	_____
_____	_____	_____
_____	_____	_____

Step 3. DEA: Delegate, Eliminate, and Automate.

- **Delegate:** Delegate any item possible to your team.
- **Eliminate:** Strikethrough any item that doesn't meet Pareto's Principle: 20% of your action creates 80% of your results.
- **Automate:** Write an "A" next to any items that you can use a system to automate.

DAILY SECTION

PREPARE & PLAN™ (AM)

Five Things I'm Grateful for Today...

1. _____
2. _____
3. _____
4. _____
5. _____

☐ **3x3**

How I want to **show up** today in one word:

_____

How I want to **feel** today in one word:

_____

If I only **got one thing done today,** it must be:

_____

5 AM	
6 AM	
7 AM	
8 AM	
9 AM	
10 AM	
11 AM	
12 PM	
1 PM	
2 PM	
3 PM	
4 PM	
5 PM	
6 PM	
7 PM	
8 PM	
9 PM	

DAILY SECTION

REFLECT & RESET™ (PM)

I drank _____ ounces of water.   I moved my body for _____ minutes.

Something I realized or a lesson I learned today: _____

_____

Something that happened today that I really appreciated: _____

_____

☐ Shut off all electronics 30 minutes before bed.

Accomplishments:

_____

_____

_____

_____

_____

Plans for Tomorrow:

_____

_____

_____

_____

_____

Notes

_____

_____

DAILY SECTION

PREPARE & PLAN™ (AM)

Five Things I'm Grateful for Today...

1. _____
2. _____
3. _____
4. _____
5. _____

☐ **3x3**

How I want to **show up** today in one word:

_____

How I want to **feel** today in one word:

_____

If I only **got one thing done today,** it must be:

_____

5 AM	
6 AM	
7 AM	
8 AM	
9 AM	
10 AM	
11 AM	
12 PM	
1 PM	
2 PM	
3 PM	
4 PM	
5 PM	
6 PM	
7 PM	
8 PM	
9 PM	

DAILY SECTION

REFLECT & RESET™ (PM)

I drank _____ ounces of water. I moved my body for _____ minutes.

Something I realized or a lesson I learned today: _____

_____

Something that happened today that I really appreciated: _____

_____

☐ Shut off all electronics 30 minutes before bed.

Accomplishments:

_____

_____

_____

_____

_____

Plans for Tomorrow:

_____

_____

_____

_____

_____

Notes

_____

_____

DAILY SECTION

PREPARE & PLAN™ (AM)

Five Things I'm Grateful for Today...

1. _____
2. _____
3. _____
4. _____
5. _____

☐ **3x3**

How I want to **show up** today in one word:

_____

How I want to **feel** today in one word:

_____

If I only **got one thing done today,** it must be:

_____

5 AM	
6 AM	
7 AM	
8 AM	
9 AM	
10 AM	
11 AM	
12 PM	
1 PM	
2 PM	
3 PM	
4 PM	
5 PM	
6 PM	
7 PM	
8 PM	
9 PM	

DAILY SECTION

REFLECT & RESET™ (PM)

I drank _____ ounces of water. I moved my body for _____ minutes.

Something I realized or a lesson I learned today: _____
_____

Something that happened today that I really appreciated: _____
_____

☐ Shut off all electronics 30 minutes before bed.

Accomplishments:

_____
_____
_____
_____
_____

Plans for Tomorrow:

_____
_____
_____
_____
_____

Notes

_____
_____

DAILY SECTION

PREPARE & PLAN™ (AM)

Five Things I'm Grateful for Today...

1. _____
2. _____
3. _____
4. _____
5. _____

☐ **3x3**

How I want to **show up** today in one word:
_____

How I want to **feel** today in one word:
_____

If I only **got one thing done today,** it must be:
_____

5 AM
6 AM
7 AM
8 AM
9 AM
10 AM
11 AM
12 PM
1 PM
2 PM
3 PM
4 PM
5 PM
6 PM
7 PM
8 PM
9 PM

DAILY SECTION

REFLECT & RESET™ (PM)

💧 I drank _____ ounces of water.   🏋️ I moved my body for _____ minutes.

Something I realized or a lesson I learned today: _____

_____

Something that happened today that I really appreciated: _____

_____

☐ Shut off all electronics 30 minutes before bed.

Accomplishments:

_____

_____

_____

_____

_____

Plans for Tomorrow:

_____

_____

_____

_____

_____

Notes

_____

_____

DAILY SECTION

PREPARE & PLAN™ (AM)

Five Things I'm Grateful for Today...

1. _____
2. _____
3. _____
4. _____
5. _____

☐ **3x3**

How I want to **show up** today in one word:
_____

How I want to **feel** today in one word:
_____

If I only **got one thing done today,** it must be:
_____

5 AM
6 AM
7 AM
8 AM
9 AM
10 AM
11 AM
12 PM
1 PM
2 PM
3 PM
4 PM
5 PM
6 PM
7 PM
8 PM
9 PM

DAILY SECTION

REFLECT & RESET™ (PM)

💧 I drank _____ ounces of water.   🏋 I moved my body for _____ minutes.

Something I realized or a lesson I learned today: _____
_____

Something that happened today that I really appreciated: _____
_____

☐ Shut off all electronics 30 minutes before bed.

Accomplishments:

_____
_____
_____
_____
_____

Plans for Tomorrow:

_____
_____
_____
_____
_____

Notes

_____
_____

MONTH

2

"**SUCCESS** IN BUSINESS IS DETERMINED BY YOUR ABILITY TO **ACQUIRE** NEW CUSTOMERS AND **RETAIN** THEM FOR THE **LONG TERM.**"

— Candy Valentino

MONTH 2

Step 1. The monthly goal review.

Refer back to your last month's goal. Analyze your progress below:

KPI	Target	Actual Result	Difference

What were your wins this month? _____
_____
_____

What gave you the most trouble this month? _____
_____
_____

What do you want to improve for next month? _____
_____

Step 2. Set next month's goal.

Refer back to your Quarterly Goal. Rewrite it below:

I will increase my _____ from _____ to _____
_____

What three KPIs would best track that goal?

KPI	Current Result	Target Result	Who Is Responsible

MONTH 2

MM _____ DD _____ YR _____ QQ _____

STATE OF THE UNION MEETING

The State of the Union Meeting is the best way to master your finances and radically change your business. During this two-hour meeting, you simply review the numbers from the prior month. For example, if today is November 8, you'll review October 1–31.

To learn more about the State of the Union Meeting, go to Chapter 7 of *The 9% Edge* and/or *The Candy Valentino Show*, available wherever you listen to podcasts.

Step 1. Prepare for your State of the Union Meeting.

- [ ] **Prepare (or have your bookkeeper prepare) the required business financial documents.**
  - [ ] These three critical business statements with three time periods each, for a total of nine:
    - [ ] **Financial Reports:** Income Statement, Cash Flow Statement, Balance Sheet
    - [ ] **Time Periods:** Monthly, Quarter to Date Comparison, Year to Date Comparison
  - [ ] Business Bank Statements for the month
  - [ ] Current Bank Reconciliations for the month
  - [ ] Business Software Reports
- [ ] **Block out two hours with a change of environment. You want to be in a different location from your normal working hours, where you are comfortable and productive.**

Step 2. Execute your State of the Union Meeting.

- [ ] **Determine if you need to hold meeting minutes based on your state and business structure. If so, take notes on your findings from this meeting.**
- [ ] **Analyze your documents.**
- [ ] **Use Financial Ratios to measure the data.**
- [ ] **Ask yourself the following questions:**
  - [ ] **People:** Do you need to establish performance reviews with any of your team members?
  - [ ] **Profit:** Do you need to run a profit optimization on your expenses?
  - [ ] **Process:** Do you need to create a process or system around any task that you're doing repetitively?

Step 3. Determine why this goal is important to you. And why now?

Based on your State of the Union Meeting, do you need to revise your KPIs for the coming month? If so, how? _____

_____

- [ ] Delegate and calendar necessary actions.

MONTH 2

Let Go of Bad Customers

To create more profit now, you also have to "let go" now. Identify the bottom 20% of your clients, so that you can go get 20% more of your best clients.

Step 1. Identify, using data, the 20% of clients who are the least profitable.

Are each of your customer relationships contributing to value?

1. Pull a report showing your customers and their sales volumes.

2. Determine the gross profitability of each of your customers, and re-sort the report to reflect a top-to-bottom order of profitability.

3. Look at the bottom 20% of customers. Calculate how much gross profit (total dollars) that these 20% represent for your company.

How to Calculate Your Gross Profit (GP)

Gross Profit is the amount of money left over after you pay for the direct expenses of making and distributing the products or services you offer.

PRICE	−	COST TO MAKE THE PRODUCT OR SERVICE	−	COST TO DISTRIBUTE THE PRODUCT OR SERVICE	=	GROSS PROFIT (GP)

PRICE		COST TO MAKE THE PRODUCT OR SERVICE		COST TO DISTRIBUTE THE PRODUCT OR SERVICE		GROSS PROFIT (GP)
☐	−	☐	−	☐	=	☐

WEEK 1

Step 1. Capture and Collect any task or idea that's on your mind.

Simply transfer these items out of your head and onto the page. This is especially important as you consider your Monthly Goals and KPIs. What do you need to do this week to be successful?

CAPTURE   &   COLLECT

"If you make customer experience a priority, you make customer acquisition irrelevant."

— Candy Valentino

WEEK 1

Step 2. Categorize your tasks or ideas.

Group like tasks or ideas together to create easier visualization and execution.

CATEGORIZE

Category:
_____
_____
_____
_____
_____
_____

Category:
_____
_____
_____
_____
_____
_____

Category:
_____
_____
_____
_____
_____
_____

Category:
_____
_____
_____
_____
_____

Category:
_____
_____
_____
_____
_____

Category:
_____
_____
_____
_____
_____

Step 3. DEA: Delegate, Eliminate, and Automate.

- **Delegate:** Delegate any item possible to your team.
- **Eliminate:** Strikethrough any item that doesn't meet Pareto's Principle: 20% of your action creates 80% of your results.
- **Automate:** Write an "A" next to any items that you can use a system to automate.

DAILY SECTION

PREPARE & PLAN™ (AM)

Five Things I'm Grateful for Today...

1. _____
2. _____
3. _____
4. _____
5. _____

☐ 3x3

How I want to **show up** today in one word:
_____

How I want to **feel** today in one word:
_____

If I only **got one thing done today,** it must be:
_____

5 AM	
6 AM	
7 AM	
8 AM	
9 AM	
10 AM	
11 AM	
12 PM	
1 PM	
2 PM	
3 PM	
4 PM	
5 PM	
6 PM	
7 PM	
8 PM	
9 PM	

DAILY SECTION

REFLECT & RESET™ (PM)

💧 I drank _____ ounces of water. 🏋 I moved my body for _____ minutes.

Something I realized or a lesson I learned today: _____

_____

Something that happened today that I really appreciated: _____

_____

☐ Shut off all electronics 30 minutes before bed.

Accomplishments:

_____

_____

_____

_____

Plans for Tomorrow:

_____

_____

_____

_____

Notes

_____

_____

DAILY SECTION

PREPARE & PLAN™ (AM)

Five Things I'm Grateful for Today...

1. _____
2. _____
3. _____
4. _____
5. _____

☐ **3x3**

How I want to **show up** today in one word:
_____

How I want to **feel** today in one word:
_____

If I only **got one thing done today,** it must be:
_____

5 AM
6 AM
7 AM
8 AM
9 AM
10 AM
11 AM
12 PM
1 PM
2 PM
3 PM
4 PM
5 PM
6 PM
7 PM
8 PM
9 PM

DAILY SECTION

REFLECT & RESET™ (PM)

I drank _____ ounces of water.   I moved my body for _____ minutes.

Something I realized or a lesson I learned today: _____
_____

Something that happened today that I really appreciated: _____
_____

☐ Shut off all electronics 30 minutes before bed.

Accomplishments:

_____
_____
_____
_____
_____

Plans for Tomorrow:

_____
_____
_____
_____

Notes

_____
_____

DAILY SECTION

MM _____ DD _____ YR _____ QQ _____

PREPARE & PLAN™ (AM)

Five Things I'm Grateful for Today...

1. _____
2. _____
3. _____
4. _____
5. _____

☐ **3x3**

How I want to **show up** today in one word:

_____

How I want to **feel** today in one word:

_____

If I only **got one thing done today,** it must be:

_____

5 AM	
6 AM	
7 AM	
8 AM	
9 AM	
10 AM	
11 AM	
12 PM	
1 PM	
2 PM	
3 PM	
4 PM	
5 PM	
6 PM	
7 PM	
8 PM	
9 PM	

DAILY SECTION

REFLECT & RESET™ (PM)

I drank _____ ounces of water.   I moved my body for _____ minutes.

Something I realized or a lesson I learned today: _____
_____

Something that happened today that I really appreciated: _____
_____

☐ Shut off all electronics 30 minutes before bed.

Accomplishments:

_____
_____
_____
_____
_____

Plans for Tomorrow:

_____
_____
_____
_____
_____

Notes

_____
_____

DAILY SECTION

PREPARE & PLAN™ (AM)

Five Things I'm Grateful for Today...

1. _____
2. _____
3. _____
4. _____
5. _____

☐ 3x3

How I want to **show up** today in one word:
_____

How I want to **feel** today in one word:
_____

If I only **got one thing done today,** it must be:
_____

| 5 AM |
| 6 AM |
| 7 AM |
| 8 AM |
| 9 AM |
| 10 AM |
| 11 AM |
| 12 PM |
| 1 PM |
| 2 PM |
| 3 PM |
| 4 PM |
| 5 PM |
| 6 PM |
| 7 PM |
| 8 PM |
| 9 PM |

DAILY SECTION

REFLECT & RESET™ (PM)

💧 I drank _____ ounces of water.   🏋️ I moved my body for _____ minutes.

Something I realized or a lesson I learned today: _____
_____

Something that happened today that I really appreciated: _____
_____

☐ Shut off all electronics 30 minutes before bed.

Accomplishments:

_____
_____
_____
_____
_____

Plans for Tomorrow:

_____
_____
_____
_____

Notes

_____
_____

DAILY SECTION

PREPARE & PLAN™ (AM)

Five Things I'm Grateful for Today...

1. _____
2. _____
3. _____
4. _____
5. _____

☐ 3x3

How I want to **show up** today in one word:

_____

How I want to **feel** today in one word:

_____

If I only **got one thing done today,** it must be:

_____

5 AM	
6 AM	
7 AM	
8 AM	
9 AM	
10 AM	
11 AM	
12 PM	
1 PM	
2 PM	
3 PM	
4 PM	
5 PM	
6 PM	
7 PM	
8 PM	
9 PM	

DAILY SECTION

_____

REFLECT & RESET™ (PM)

🌢 I drank _____ ounces of water.   🏋 I moved my body for _____ minutes.

Something I realized or a lesson I learned today: _____

_____

Something that happened today that I really appreciated: _____

_____

☐ Shut off all electronics 30 minutes before bed.

Accomplishments:

_____
_____
_____
_____
_____

Plans for Tomorrow:

_____
_____
_____
_____

Notes

_____
_____

WEEK 2

Step 1. Capture and Collect any task or idea that's on your mind.

Simply transfer these items out of your head and onto the page. This is especially important as you consider your Monthly Goals and KPIs. What do you need to do this week to be successful?

CAPTURE & **COLLECT**

"Ignorance isn't bliss. Ignorance is damn expensive."

— Candy Valentino

WEEK 2

Step 2. Categorize your tasks or ideas.

Group like tasks or ideas together to create easier visualization and execution.

CATEGORIZE

Category:

_____
_____
_____
_____
_____
_____

Category:

_____
_____
_____
_____
_____
_____

Category:

_____
_____
_____
_____
_____
_____

Category:

_____
_____
_____
_____
_____
_____

Category:

_____
_____
_____
_____
_____
_____

Category:

_____
_____
_____
_____
_____
_____

Step 3. DEA: Delegate, Eliminate, and Automate.

- **Delegate:** Delegate any item possible to your team.
- **Eliminate:** Strikethrough any item that doesn't meet Pareto's Principle: 20% of your action creates 80% of your results.
- **Automate:** Write an "A" next to any items that you can use a system to automate.

DAILY SECTION

PREPARE & PLAN™ (AM)

Five Things I'm Grateful for Today...

1. _____
2. _____
3. _____
4. _____
5. _____

☐ **3x3**

How I want to **show up** today in one word:

_____

How I want to **feel** today in one word:

_____

If I only **got one thing done today,** it must be:

_____

5 AM
6 AM
7 AM
8 AM
9 AM
10 AM
11 AM
12 PM
1 PM
2 PM
3 PM
4 PM
5 PM
6 PM
7 PM
8 PM
9 PM

DAILY SECTION

REFLECT & RESET™ (PM)

I drank _____ ounces of water.   I moved my body for _____ minutes.

Something I realized or a lesson I learned today: _____

_____

Something that happened today that I really appreciated: _____

_____

☐ Shut off all electronics 30 minutes before bed.

Accomplishments:

_____

_____

_____

_____

_____

Plans for Tomorrow:

_____

_____

_____

_____

_____

Notes

_____

_____

DAILY SECTION

PREPARE & PLAN™ (AM)

Five Things I'm Grateful for Today...

1. _____
2. _____
3. _____
4. _____
5. _____

☐ 3x3

How I want to **show up** today in one word:
_____

How I want to **feel** today in one word:
_____

If I only **got one thing done today,** it must be:
_____

5 AM
6 AM
7 AM
8 AM
9 AM
10 AM
11 AM
12 PM
1 PM
2 PM
3 PM
4 PM
5 PM
6 PM
7 PM
8 PM
9 PM

DAILY SECTION

REFLECT & RESET™ (PM)

💧 I drank _____ ounces of water.   🏋 I moved my body for _____ minutes.

Something I realized or a lesson I learned today: _____

_____

Something that happened today that I really appreciated: _____

_____

☐ Shut off all electronics 30 minutes before bed.

Accomplishments:

Plans for Tomorrow:

Notes

DAILY SECTION

MM _____ DD _____ YR _____ QQ _____

PREPARE & PLAN™ (AM)

Five Things I'm Grateful for Today...

1. _____
2. _____
3. _____
4. _____
5. _____

☐ **3x3**

How I want to **show up** today in one word:
_____

How I want to **feel** today in one word:
_____

If I only **got one thing done today,** it must be:
_____

5 AM	
6 AM	
7 AM	
8 AM	
9 AM	
10 AM	
11 AM	
12 PM	
1 PM	
2 PM	
3 PM	
4 PM	
5 PM	
6 PM	
7 PM	
8 PM	
9 PM	

DAILY SECTION

REFLECT & RESET™ (PM)

💧 I drank _____ ounces of water.　　🏋 I moved my body for _____ minutes.

Something I realized or a lesson I learned today: _____

_____

Something that happened today that I really appreciated: _____

_____

☐ Shut off all electronics 30 minutes before bed.

Accomplishments:

_____

_____

_____

_____

_____

Plans for Tomorrow:

_____

_____

_____

_____

_____

Notes

_____

_____

DAILY SECTION

PREPARE & PLAN™ (AM)

Five Things I'm Grateful for Today...

1. _____
2. _____
3. _____
4. _____
5. _____

☐ **3x3**

How I want to **show up** today in one word:
_____

How I want to **feel** today in one word:
_____

If I only **got one thing done today,** it must be:
_____

5 AM	
6 AM	
7 AM	
8 AM	
9 AM	
10 AM	
11 AM	
12 PM	
1 PM	
2 PM	
3 PM	
4 PM	
5 PM	
6 PM	
7 PM	
8 PM	
9 PM	

DAILY SECTION

REFLECT & RESET™ (PM)

I drank _____ ounces of water. I moved my body for _____ minutes.

Something I realized or a lesson I learned today: _____
_____

Something that happened today that I really appreciated: _____
_____

☐ Shut off all electronics 30 minutes before bed.

Accomplishments:

_____
_____
_____
_____
_____

Plans for Tomorrow:

_____
_____
_____
_____
_____

Notes

_____
_____

DAILY SECTION

MM _____ DD _____ YR _____ QQ _____

PREPARE & PLAN™ (AM)

Five Things I'm Grateful for Today...

1. _____
2. _____
3. _____
4. _____
5. _____

☐ 3x3

How I want to **show up** today in one word:

_____

How I want to **feel** today in one word:

_____

If I only **got one thing done today,** it must be:

_____

| 5 AM |
| 6 AM |
| 7 AM |
| 8 AM |
| 9 AM |
| 10 AM |
| 11 AM |
| 12 PM |
| 1 PM |
| 2 PM |
| 3 PM |
| 4 PM |
| 5 PM |
| 6 PM |
| 7 PM |
| 8 PM |
| 9 PM |

DAILY SECTION

_____

REFLECT & RESET™ (PM)

💧 I drank _____ ounces of water.   🏋 I moved my body for _____ minutes.

Something I realized or a lesson I learned today: _____

_____

Something that happened today that I really appreciated: _____

_____

☐ Shut off all electronics 30 minutes before bed.

Accomplishments:

_____
_____
_____
_____
_____

Plans for Tomorrow:

_____
_____
_____
_____
_____

Notes

_____
_____

WEEK 3

Step 1. Capture and Collect any task or idea that's on your mind.

Simply transfer these items out of your head and onto the page. This is especially important as you consider your Monthly Goals and KPIs. What do you need to do this week to be successful?

CAPTURE & COLLECT

"No one will care about your bottom line more than you."

— Candy Valentino

WEEK 3

Step 2. Categorize your tasks or ideas.

Group like tasks or ideas together to create easier visualization and execution.

CATEGORIZE

Category:

_____
_____
_____
_____
_____
_____

Category:

_____
_____
_____
_____
_____
_____

Category:

_____
_____
_____
_____
_____
_____

Category:

_____
_____
_____
_____
_____
_____

Category:

_____
_____
_____
_____
_____
_____

Category:

_____
_____
_____
_____
_____
_____

Step 3. DEA: Delegate, Eliminate, and Automate.

- **Delegate:** Delegate any item possible to your team.
- **Eliminate:** Strikethrough any item that doesn't meet Pareto's Principle: 20% of your action creates 80% of your results.
- **Automate:** Write an "A" next to any items that you can use a system to automate.

DAILY SECTION

MM _____ DD _____ YR _____ QQ _____

PREPARE & PLAN™ (AM)

Five Things I'm Grateful for Today...

1. _____
2. _____
3. _____
4. _____
5. _____

☐ **3x3**

How I want to **show up** today in one word:

_____

How I want to **feel** today in one word:

_____

If I only **got one thing done today,** it must be:

_____

5 AM	
6 AM	
7 AM	
8 AM	
9 AM	
10 AM	
11 AM	
12 PM	
1 PM	
2 PM	
3 PM	
4 PM	
5 PM	
6 PM	
7 PM	
8 PM	
9 PM	

DAILY SECTION

REFLECT & RESET™ (PM)

💧 I drank _____ ounces of water.   🏋 I moved my body for _____ minutes.

Something I realized or a lesson I learned today: _____

_____

Something that happened today that I really appreciated: _____

_____

☐ Shut off all electronics 30 minutes before bed.

Accomplishments:

_____

_____

_____

_____

_____

Plans for Tomorrow:

_____

_____

_____

_____

_____

Notes

_____

_____

DAILY SECTION

PREPARE & PLAN™ (AM)

Five Things I'm Grateful for Today...

1. _____
2. _____
3. _____
4. _____
5. _____

☐ **3x3**

How I want to **show up** today in one word:
_____

How I want to **feel** today in one word:
_____

If I only **got one thing done today,** it must be:
_____

5 AM	
6 AM	
7 AM	
8 AM	
9 AM	
10 AM	
11 AM	
12 PM	
1 PM	
2 PM	
3 PM	
4 PM	
5 PM	
6 PM	
7 PM	
8 PM	
9 PM	

DAILY SECTION

REFLECT & RESET™ (PM)

💧 I drank _____ ounces of water. 🏋 I moved my body for _____ minutes.

Something I realized or a lesson I learned today: _____

_____

Something that happened today that I really appreciated: _____

_____

☐ Shut off all electronics 30 minutes before bed.

Accomplishments:

_____

_____

_____

_____

Plans for Tomorrow:

_____

_____

_____

_____

Notes

_____

_____

DAILY SECTION

MM _____ DD _____ YR _____ QQ _____

_____

PREPARE & PLAN™ (AM)

Five Things I'm Grateful for Today...

1. _____
2. _____
3. _____
4. _____
5. _____

☐ **3x3**

How I want to **show up** today in one word:
_____

How I want to **feel** today in one word:
_____

If I only **got one thing done today,** it must be:
_____

5 AM	
6 AM	
7 AM	
8 AM	
9 AM	
10 AM	
11 AM	
12 PM	
1 PM	
2 PM	
3 PM	
4 PM	
5 PM	
6 PM	
7 PM	
8 PM	
9 PM	

DAILY SECTION

REFLECT & RESET™ (PM)

💧 I drank _____ ounces of water.   🏋 I moved my body for _____ minutes.

Something I realized or a lesson I learned today: _____

_____

Something that happened today that I really appreciated: _____

_____

☐ Shut off all electronics 30 minutes before bed.

Accomplishments:

_____
_____
_____
_____
_____

Plans for Tomorrow:

_____
_____
_____
_____
_____

Notes

_____
_____

DAILY SECTION

PREPARE & PLAN™ (AM)

Five Things I'm Grateful for Today...

1. _____
2. _____
3. _____
4. _____
5. _____

☐ 3x3

How I want to **show up** today in one word:

_____

How I want to **feel** today in one word:

_____

If I only **got one thing done today,** it must be:

_____

5 AM	
6 AM	
7 AM	
8 AM	
9 AM	
10 AM	
11 AM	
12 PM	
1 PM	
2 PM	
3 PM	
4 PM	
5 PM	
6 PM	
7 PM	
8 PM	
9 PM	

DAILY SECTION

REFLECT & RESET™ (PM)

💧 I drank _____ ounces of water. 🏋 I moved my body for _____ minutes.

Something I realized or a lesson I learned today: _____

_____

Something that happened today that I really appreciated: _____

_____

☐ Shut off all electronics 30 minutes before bed.

Accomplishments:

_____

_____

_____

_____

_____

Plans for Tomorrow:

_____

_____

_____

_____

_____

Notes

_____

_____

DAILY SECTION

MM _____ DD _____ YR _____ QQ _____

PREPARE & PLAN™ (AM)

Five Things I'm Grateful for Today...

1. _____
2. _____
3. _____
4. _____
5. _____

☐ **3x3**

How I want to **show up** today in one word:
_____

How I want to **feel** today in one word:
_____

If I only **got one thing done today,** it must be:
_____

5 AM
6 AM
7 AM
8 AM
9 AM
10 AM
11 AM
12 PM
1 PM
2 PM
3 PM
4 PM
5 PM
6 PM
7 PM
8 PM
9 PM

DAILY SECTION

REFLECT & RESET™ (PM)

I drank _____ ounces of water.   I moved my body for _____ minutes.

Something I realized or a lesson I learned today: _____

_____

Something that happened today that I really appreciated: _____

_____

☐ Shut off all electronics 30 minutes before bed.

Accomplishments:

_____

_____

_____

_____

_____

Plans for Tomorrow:

_____

_____

_____

_____

_____

Notes

_____

_____

WEEK 4

Step 1. Capture and Collect any task or idea that's on your mind.

Simply transfer these items out of your head and onto the page. This is especially important as you consider your Monthly Goals and KPIs. What do you need to do this week to be successful?

CAPTURE & COLLECT

"The more accurate your financial statements are, the more informed decisions you'll be able to make to grow and scale your business."

— Candy Valentino

WEEK 4

Step 2. Categorize your tasks or ideas.

Group like tasks or ideas together to create easier visualization and execution.

CATEGORIZE

Category:
_____
_____
_____
_____
_____
_____

Category:
_____
_____
_____
_____
_____
_____

Category:
_____
_____
_____
_____
_____
_____

Category:
_____
_____
_____
_____
_____
_____

Category:
_____
_____
_____
_____
_____
_____

Category:
_____
_____
_____
_____
_____
_____

Step 3. DEA: Delegate, Eliminate, and Automate.

- **Delegate:** Delegate any item possible to your team.
- **Eliminate:** Strikethrough any item that doesn't meet Pareto's Principle: 20% of your action creates 80% of your results.
- **Automate:** Write an "A" next to any items that you can use a system to automate.

DAILY SECTION

MM _____ DD _____ YR _____ QQ _____

_____

PREPARE & PLAN™ (AM)

Five Things I'm Grateful for Today...

1. _____
2. _____
3. _____
4. _____
5. _____

☐ **3x3**

How I want to **show up** today in one word:

_____

How I want to **feel** today in one word:

_____

If I only **got one thing done today,** it must be:

_____

5 AM	
6 AM	
7 AM	
8 AM	
9 AM	
10 AM	
11 AM	
12 PM	
1 PM	
2 PM	
3 PM	
4 PM	
5 PM	
6 PM	
7 PM	
8 PM	
9 PM	

DAILY SECTION

_____

REFLECT & RESET™ (PM)

💧 I drank _____ ounces of water.   🏋️ I moved my body for _____ minutes.

Something I realized or a lesson I learned today: _____

_____

Something that happened today that I really appreciated: _____

_____

☐ Shut off all electronics 30 minutes before bed.

Accomplishments:

_____
_____
_____
_____
_____

Plans for Tomorrow:

_____
_____
_____
_____
_____

Notes

_____
_____

DAILY SECTION

PREPARE & PLAN™ (AM)

Five Things I'm Grateful for Today...

1. _____
2. _____
3. _____
4. _____
5. _____

☐ **3x3**

How I want to **show up** today in one word:
_____

How I want to **feel** today in one word:
_____

If I only **got one thing done today,** it must be:
_____

5 AM
6 AM
7 AM
8 AM
9 AM
10 AM
11 AM
12 PM
1 PM
2 PM
3 PM
4 PM
5 PM
6 PM
7 PM
8 PM
9 PM

DAILY SECTION

REFLECT & RESET™ (PM)

💧 I drank _____ ounces of water.   🏋 I moved my body for _____ minutes.

Something I realized or a lesson I learned today: _____

_____

Something that happened today that I really appreciated: _____

_____

☐ Shut off all electronics 30 minutes before bed.

Accomplishments:

_____
_____
_____
_____
_____

Plans for Tomorrow:

_____
_____
_____
_____
_____

Notes

_____
_____

DAILY SECTION

PREPARE & PLAN™ (AM)

Five Things I'm Grateful for Today...

1. _____
2. _____
3. _____
4. _____
5. _____

☐ **3x3**

How I want to **show up** today in one word:
_____

How I want to **feel** today in one word:
_____

If I only **got one thing done today,** it must be:
_____

5 AM	
6 AM	
7 AM	
8 AM	
9 AM	
10 AM	
11 AM	
12 PM	
1 PM	
2 PM	
3 PM	
4 PM	
5 PM	
6 PM	
7 PM	
8 PM	
9 PM	

DAILY SECTION

REFLECT & RESET™ (PM)

💧 I drank _____ ounces of water.   🏋️ I moved my body for _____ minutes.

Something I realized or a lesson I learned today: _____

_____

Something that happened today that I really appreciated: _____

_____

☐ Shut off all electronics 30 minutes before bed.

Accomplishments:

_____

_____

_____

_____

_____

Plans for Tomorrow:

_____

_____

_____

_____

_____

Notes

_____

_____

DAILY SECTION

PREPARE & PLAN™ (AM)

Five Things I'm Grateful for Today...

1. _____
2. _____
3. _____
4. _____
5. _____

☐ **3x3**

How I want to **show up** today in one word:
_____

How I want to **feel** today in one word:
_____

If I only **got one thing done today,** it must be:
_____

5 AM	
6 AM	
7 AM	
8 AM	
9 AM	
10 AM	
11 AM	
12 PM	
1 PM	
2 PM	
3 PM	
4 PM	
5 PM	
6 PM	
7 PM	
8 PM	
9 PM	

DAILY SECTION

REFLECT & RESET™ (PM)

I drank _____ ounces of water.   I moved my body for _____ minutes.

Something I realized or a lesson I learned today: _____

_____

Something that happened today that I really appreciated: _____

_____

☐ Shut off all electronics 30 minutes before bed.

Accomplishments:

_____

_____

_____

_____

_____

Plans for Tomorrow:

_____

_____

_____

_____

_____

Notes

_____

_____

DAILY SECTION

PREPARE & PLAN™ (AM)

Five Things I'm Grateful for Today...

1. _____
2. _____
3. _____
4. _____
5. _____

☐ **3x3**

How I want to **show up** today in one word:
_____

How I want to **feel** today in one word:
_____

If I only **got one thing done today,** it must be:
_____

5 AM	
6 AM	
7 AM	
8 AM	
9 AM	
10 AM	
11 AM	
12 PM	
1 PM	
2 PM	
3 PM	
4 PM	
5 PM	
6 PM	
7 PM	
8 PM	
9 PM	

DAILY SECTION

REFLECT & RESET™ (PM)

💧 I drank _____ ounces of water.　🏋 I moved my body for _____ minutes.

Something I realized or a lesson I learned today: _____

_____

Something that happened today that I really appreciated: _____

_____

☐ Shut off all electronics 30 minutes before bed.

Accomplishments:

_____

_____

_____

_____

Plans for Tomorrow:

_____

_____

_____

_____

Notes

_____

_____

MONTH

3

"IF YOU **SET OFF** WITHOUT A **PLAN**, IT'S LIKE GETTING IN THE CAR WITHOUT HAVING A **DESTINATION.**"

— **Candy Valentino**

MONTH 3

MM _____ DD _____ YR _____ QQ _____

Step 1. The monthly goal review.

Refer back to your last month's goal. Analyze your progress below:

KPI	Target	Actual Result	Difference

What were your wins this month? _____
_____
_____

What gave you the most trouble this month? _____
_____
_____

What do you want to improve for next month? _____
_____

Step 2. Set next month's goal.

Refer back to your Quarterly Goal. Rewrite it below:

I will increase my _____ from _____ to _____
_____

What three KPIs would best track that goal?

KPI	Current Result	Target Result	Who Is Responsible

MONTH 3

STATE OF THE UNION MEETING

The State of the Union Meeting is the best way to master your finances and radically change your business. During this two-hour meeting, you simply review the numbers from the prior month. For example, if today is November 8, you'll review October 1–31.

To learn more about the State of the Union Meeting, go to Chapter 7 of *The 9% Edge* and/or *The Candy Valentino Show*, available wherever you listen to podcasts.

Step 1. Prepare for your State of the Union Meeting.

- [ ] **Prepare (or have your bookkeeper prepare) the required business financial documents.**
  - [ ] These three critical business statements with three time periods each, for a total of nine:
    - [ ] **Financial Reports:** Income Statement, Cash Flow Statement, Balance Sheet
    - [ ] **Time Periods:** Monthly, Quarter to Date Comparison, Year to Date Comparison
  - [ ] Business Bank Statements for the month
  - [ ] Current Bank Reconciliations for the month
  - [ ] Business Software Reports
- [ ] **Block out two hours with a change of environment. You want to be in a different location from your normal working hours, where you are comfortable and productive.**

Step 2. Execute your State of the Union Meeting.

- [ ] **Determine if you need to hold meeting minutes based on your state and business structure. If so, take notes on your findings from this meeting.**
- [ ] **Analyze your documents.**
- [ ] **Use Financial Ratios to measure the data.**
- [ ] **Ask yourself the following questions:**
  - [ ] **People:** Do you need to establish performance reviews with any of your team members?
  - [ ] **Profit:** Do you need to run a profit optimization on your expenses?
  - [ ] **Process:** Do you need to create a process or system around any task that you're doing repetitively?

Step 3. Determine why this goal is important to you. And why now?

Based on your State of the Union Meeting, do you need to revise your KPIs for the coming month? If so, how? _____

_____

- [ ] Delegate and calendar necessary actions.

MONTH 3

Duplicate your top customers.

Regardless of your industry and what kind of customers you serve, if you replaced 20% of your worst-performing customers with 20% more of your best-performing customers, what results would you see?

Step 1. Identify, using data, the 20% of clients who are the most profitable.

Finding *Your* Best Customers

☐ Log into your POS, CRM, e-commerce platform, or software system where you keep sales and customer data.

☐ Review an annual report of customer data, including purchases, interactions, and demographics.

☐ Utilize your system's segmentation tools to categorize customers by their total spend, frequency of purchases, and level of engagement.

☐ Focus on the top segments and analyze them for common characteristics, such as demographics, purchasing behavior, product preferences, and how they engage with your business.

☐ Based on your findings, draft a profile of your ideal customer archetype. Include key attributes like age range, interests, purchasing habits, as well as preferred communication channels and what marketing channel you acquired them through.

Step 2. Find more of your top customers.

Want a list of strategies that might work for your business? Check out Chapter 8 of *The 9% Edge*.

How might you engage with these customers more? _____

_____

_____

WEEK 1

Step 1. Capture and Collect any task or idea that's on your mind.

Simply transfer these items out of your head and onto the page. This is especially important as you consider your Monthly Goals and KPIs. What do you need to do this week to be successful?

CAPTURE & COLLECT

"Your exit will likely end up different than you expect, but it may end up being exactly what you need."

— Candy Valentino

Step 2. Categorize your tasks or ideas.

Group like tasks or ideas together to create easier visualization and execution.

CATEGORIZE

Category:	Category:	Category:
_____	_____	_____
_____	_____	_____
_____	_____	_____
_____	_____	_____
_____	_____	_____
_____	_____	_____

Category:	Category:	Category:
_____	_____	_____
_____	_____	_____
_____	_____	_____
_____	_____	_____
_____	_____	_____

Step 3. DEA: Delegate, Eliminate, and Automate.

- **Delegate:** Delegate any item possible to your team.
- **Eliminate:** Strikethrough any item that doesn't meet Pareto's Principle: 20% of your action creates 80% of your results.
- **Automate:** Write an "A" next to any items that you can use a system to automate.

DAILY SECTION

PREPARE & PLAN™ (AM)

Five Things I'm Grateful for Today...

1. _____
2. _____
3. _____
4. _____
5. _____

☐ **3x3**

How I want to **show up** today in one word:
_____

How I want to **feel** today in one word:
_____

If I only **got one thing done today,** it must be:
_____

5 AM	
6 AM	
7 AM	
8 AM	
9 AM	
10 AM	
11 AM	
12 PM	
1 PM	
2 PM	
3 PM	
4 PM	
5 PM	
6 PM	
7 PM	
8 PM	
9 PM	

DAILY SECTION

REFLECT & RESET™ (PM)

I drank _____ ounces of water.   I moved my body for _____ minutes.

Something I realized or a lesson I learned today: _____

_____

Something that happened today that I really appreciated: _____

_____

☐ Shut off all electronics 30 minutes before bed.

Accomplishments:

_____

_____

_____

_____

_____

Plans for Tomorrow:

_____

_____

_____

_____

Notes

_____

_____

DAILY SECTION

PREPARE & PLAN™ (AM)

Five Things I'm Grateful for Today...

1. _____
2. _____
3. _____
4. _____
5. _____

☐ **3x3**

How I want to **show up** today in one word:
_____

How I want to **feel** today in one word:
_____

If I only **got one thing done today,** it must be:
_____

5 AM	
6 AM	
7 AM	
8 AM	
9 AM	
10 AM	
11 AM	
12 PM	
1 PM	
2 PM	
3 PM	
4 PM	
5 PM	
6 PM	
7 PM	
8 PM	
9 PM	

DAILY SECTION

REFLECT & RESET™ (PM)

💧 I drank _____ ounces of water.   🏋 I moved my body for _____ minutes.

Something I realized or a lesson I learned today: _____
_____

Something that happened today that I really appreciated: _____
_____

☐ Shut off all electronics 30 minutes before bed.

Accomplishments:

_____
_____
_____
_____
_____

Plans for Tomorrow:

_____
_____
_____
_____

Notes

_____
_____

DAILY SECTION

MM _____ DD _____ YR _____ QQ _____

PREPARE & PLAN™ (AM)

Five Things I'm Grateful for Today...

1. _____
2. _____
3. _____
4. _____
5. _____

☐ **3x3**

How I want to **show up** today in one word:

_____

How I want to **feel** today in one word:

_____

If I only **got one thing done today,** it must be:

_____

5 AM	
6 AM	
7 AM	
8 AM	
9 AM	
10 AM	
11 AM	
12 PM	
1 PM	
2 PM	
3 PM	
4 PM	
5 PM	
6 PM	
7 PM	
8 PM	
9 PM	

DAILY SECTION

REFLECT & RESET™ (PM)

I drank _____ ounces of water. I moved my body for _____ minutes.

Something I realized or a lesson I learned today: _____
_____

Something that happened today that I really appreciated: _____
_____

☐ Shut off all electronics 30 minutes before bed.

Accomplishments:

_____
_____
_____
_____
_____

Plans for Tomorrow:

_____
_____
_____
_____
_____

Notes

_____
_____

DAILY SECTION

PREPARE & PLAN™ (AM)

Five Things I'm Grateful for Today...

1. _____
2. _____
3. _____
4. _____
5. _____

☐ **3x3**

How I want to **show up** today in one word:
_____

How I want to **feel** today in one word:
_____

If I only **got one thing done today,** it must be:
_____

5 AM	
6 AM	
7 AM	
8 AM	
9 AM	
10 AM	
11 AM	
12 PM	
1 PM	
2 PM	
3 PM	
4 PM	
5 PM	
6 PM	
7 PM	
8 PM	
9 PM	

DAILY SECTION

_____

REFLECT & RESET™ (PM)

I drank _____ ounces of water. I moved my body for _____ minutes.

Something I realized or a lesson I learned today: _____

_____

Something that happened today that I really appreciated: _____

_____

☐ Shut off all electronics 30 minutes before bed.

Accomplishments:

_____
_____
_____
_____
_____

Plans for Tomorrow:

_____
_____
_____
_____
_____

Notes

_____
_____

DAILY SECTION

PREPARE & PLAN™ (AM)

Five Things I'm Grateful for Today...

1. _____
2. _____
3. _____
4. _____
5. _____

☐ **3x3**

How I want to **show up** today in one word:
_____

How I want to **feel** today in one word:
_____

If I only **got one thing done today,** it must be:
_____

5 AM	
6 AM	
7 AM	
8 AM	
9 AM	
10 AM	
11 AM	
12 PM	
1 PM	
2 PM	
3 PM	
4 PM	
5 PM	
6 PM	
7 PM	
8 PM	
9 PM	

DAILY SECTION

REFLECT & RESET™ (PM)

I drank _____ ounces of water.   I moved my body for _____ minutes.

Something I realized or a lesson I learned today: _____

_____

Something that happened today that I really appreciated: _____

_____

☐ Shut off all electronics 30 minutes before bed.

Accomplishments:

_____

_____

_____

_____

_____

Plans for Tomorrow:

_____

_____

_____

_____

_____

Notes

_____

_____

WEEK 2

Step 1. Capture and Collect any task or idea that's on your mind.

Simply transfer these items out of your head and onto the page. This is especially important as you consider your Monthly Goals and KPIs. What do you need to do this week to be successful?

CAPTURE & COLLECT

"The more valuable you are to the business, the less valuable the business is."

— Candy Valentino

WEEK 2

Step 2. Categorize your tasks or ideas.

Group like tasks or ideas together to create easier visualization and execution.

CATEGORIZE

Category:
_____
_____
_____
_____
_____
_____

Category:
_____
_____
_____
_____
_____
_____

Category:
_____
_____
_____
_____
_____
_____

Category:
_____
_____
_____
_____
_____

Category:
_____
_____
_____
_____
_____

Category:
_____
_____
_____
_____
_____

Step 3. DEA: Delegate, Eliminate, and Automate.

- **Delegate:** Delegate any item possible to your team.
- **Eliminate:** Strikethrough any item that doesn't meet Pareto's Principle: 20% of your action creates 80% of your results.
- **Automate:** Write an "A" next to any items that you can use a system to automate.

DAILY SECTION

PREPARE & PLAN™ (AM)

Five Things I'm Grateful for Today...

1. _____
2. _____
3. _____
4. _____
5. _____

☐ **3x3**

How I want to **show up** today in one word:
_____

How I want to **feel** today in one word:
_____

If I only **got one thing done today,** it must be:
_____

5 AM	
6 AM	
7 AM	
8 AM	
9 AM	
10 AM	
11 AM	
12 PM	
1 PM	
2 PM	
3 PM	
4 PM	
5 PM	
6 PM	
7 PM	
8 PM	
9 PM	

DAILY SECTION

REFLECT & RESET™ (PM)

💧 I drank _____ ounces of water.　　🏋️ I moved my body for _____ minutes.

Something I realized or a lesson I learned today: _____
_____

Something that happened today that I really appreciated: _____
_____

☐ Shut off all electronics 30 minutes before bed.

Accomplishments:

_____
_____
_____
_____

Plans for Tomorrow:

_____
_____
_____
_____
_____

Notes

_____
_____

DAILY SECTION

MM _____ DD _____ YR _____ QQ _____

_____

PREPARE & PLAN™ (AM)

Five Things I'm Grateful for Today...

1. _____

2. _____

3. _____

4. _____

5. _____

☐ **3x3**

How I want to **show up** today in one word:

_____

How I want to **feel** today in one word:

_____

If I only **got one thing done today,** it must be:

_____

5 AM
6 AM
7 AM
8 AM
9 AM
10 AM
11 AM
12 PM
1 PM
2 PM
3 PM
4 PM
5 PM
6 PM
7 PM
8 PM
9 PM

DAILY SECTION

REFLECT & RESET™ (PM)

💧 I drank _____ ounces of water. 🏋 I moved my body for _____ minutes.

Something I realized or a lesson I learned today: _____
_____

Something that happened today that I really appreciated: _____
_____

☐ Shut off all electronics 30 minutes before bed.

Accomplishments:

_____
_____
_____
_____
_____

Plans for Tomorrow:

_____
_____
_____
_____

Notes

_____
_____

DAILY SECTION

PREPARE & PLAN™ (AM)

Five Things I'm Grateful for Today...

1. _____
2. _____
3. _____
4. _____
5. _____

☐ **3x3**

How I want to **show up** today in one word:
_____

How I want to **feel** today in one word:
_____

If I only **got one thing done today,** it must be:
_____

5 AM	
6 AM	
7 AM	
8 AM	
9 AM	
10 AM	
11 AM	
12 PM	
1 PM	
2 PM	
3 PM	
4 PM	
5 PM	
6 PM	
7 PM	
8 PM	
9 PM	

DAILY SECTION

_____

REFLECT & RESET™ (PM)

⬥ I drank _____ ounces of water.   ⬛ I moved my body for _____ minutes.

Something I realized or a lesson I learned today: _____
_____

Something that happened today that I really appreciated: _____
_____

☐ Shut off all electronics 30 minutes before bed.

Accomplishments:

_____
_____
_____
_____
_____

Plans for Tomorrow:

_____
_____
_____
_____
_____

Notes

_____
_____

DAILY SECTION

MM _____ DD _____ YR _____ QQ _____

Five Things I'm Grateful for Today...

1. _____
2. _____
3. _____
4. _____
5. _____

☐ **3x3**

How I want to **show up** today in one word:

_____

How I want to **feel** today in one word:

_____

If I only **got one thing done today,** it must be:

_____

5 AM	
6 AM	
7 AM	
8 AM	
9 AM	
10 AM	
11 AM	
12 PM	
1 PM	
2 PM	
3 PM	
4 PM	
5 PM	
6 PM	
7 PM	
8 PM	
9 PM	

DAILY SECTION

REFLECT & RESET™ (PM)

💧 I drank _____ ounces of water.   🏋 I moved my body for _____ minutes.

Something I realized or a lesson I learned today: _____
_____

Something that happened today that I really appreciated: _____
_____

☐ Shut off all electronics 30 minutes before bed.

Accomplishments:

_____
_____
_____
_____
_____

Plans for Tomorrow:

_____
_____
_____
_____
_____

Notes

_____
_____

DAILY SECTION

PREPARE & PLAN™ (AM)

Five Things I'm Grateful for Today...

1. _____
2. _____
3. _____
4. _____
5. _____

☐ **3x3**

How I want to **show up** today in one word:
_____

How I want to **feel** today in one word:
_____

If I only **got one thing done today,** it must be:
_____

5 AM	
6 AM	
7 AM	
8 AM	
9 AM	
10 AM	
11 AM	
12 PM	
1 PM	
2 PM	
3 PM	
4 PM	
5 PM	
6 PM	
7 PM	
8 PM	
9 PM	

DAILY SECTION

REFLECT & RESET™ (PM)

💧 I drank _____ ounces of water.   🏋 I moved my body for _____ minutes.

Something I realized or a lesson I learned today: _____
_____

Something that happened today that I really appreciated: _____
_____

☐ Shut off all electronics 30 minutes before bed.

Accomplishments:

_____
_____
_____
_____
_____

Plans for Tomorrow:

_____
_____
_____
_____

Notes

_____
_____

WEEK 3

MM _____ DD _____ YR _____ QQ _____

Step 1. Capture and Collect any task or idea that's on your mind.

Simply transfer these items out of your head and onto the page. This is especially important as you consider your Monthly Goals and KPIs. What do you need to do this week to be successful?

CAPTURE   **&**   COLLECT

"Successful leaders are more vision-oriented, while successful managers are more detail-oriented."

— Candy Valentino

WEEK 3

Step 2. Categorize your tasks or ideas.

Group like tasks or ideas together to create easier visualization and execution.

CATEGORIZE

Category:
_____
_____
_____
_____
_____
_____

Category:
_____
_____
_____
_____
_____
_____

Category:
_____
_____
_____
_____
_____
_____

Category:
_____
_____
_____
_____
_____
_____

Category:
_____
_____
_____
_____
_____
_____

Category:
_____
_____
_____
_____
_____
_____

Step 3. DEA: Delegate, Eliminate, and Automate.

- **Delegate:** Delegate any item possible to your team.
- **Eliminate:** Strikethrough any item that doesn't meet Pareto's Principle: 20% of your action creates 80% of your results.
- **Automate:** Write an "A" next to any items that you can use a system to automate.

DAILY SECTION

MM _____ DD _____ YR _____ QQ _____

_____

PREPARE & PLAN™ (AM)

Five Things I'm Grateful for Today...

1. _____

2. _____

3. _____

4. _____

5. _____

☐ **3x3**

How I want to **show up** today in one word:

_____

How I want to **feel** today in one word:

_____

If I only **got one thing done today,** it must be:

_____

5 AM	
6 AM	
7 AM	
8 AM	
9 AM	
10 AM	
11 AM	
12 PM	
1 PM	
2 PM	
3 PM	
4 PM	
5 PM	
6 PM	
7 PM	
8 PM	
9 PM	

DAILY SECTION

MM _____ DD _____ YR _____ QQ _____

REFLECT & RESET™ (PM)

🖤 I drank _____ ounces of water.   🏋 I moved my body for _____ minutes.

Something I realized or a lesson I learned today: _____
_____

Something that happened today that I really appreciated: _____
_____

☐ Shut off all electronics 30 minutes before bed.

Accomplishments:

_____
_____
_____
_____
_____

Plans for Tomorrow:

_____
_____
_____
_____
_____

Notes

_____
_____

DAILY SECTION

PREPARE & PLAN™ (AM)

Five Things I'm Grateful for Today...

1. _____
2. _____
3. _____
4. _____
5. _____

☐ **3x3**

How I want to **show up** today in one word:
_____

How I want to **feel** today in one word:
_____

If I only **got one thing done today,** it must be:
_____

5 AM	
6 AM	
7 AM	
8 AM	
9 AM	
10 AM	
11 AM	
12 PM	
1 PM	
2 PM	
3 PM	
4 PM	
5 PM	
6 PM	
7 PM	
8 PM	
9 PM	

DAILY SECTION

REFLECT & RESET™ (PM)

💧 I drank _____ ounces of water.   🏋 I moved my body for _____ minutes.

Something I realized or a lesson I learned today: _____

_____

Something that happened today that I really appreciated: _____

_____

☐ Shut off all electronics 30 minutes before bed.

Accomplishments:

_____

_____

_____

_____

_____

Plans for Tomorrow:

_____

_____

_____

_____

_____

Notes

_____

_____

DAILY SECTION

PREPARE & PLAN™ (AM)

Five Things I'm Grateful for Today...

1. _____
2. _____
3. _____
4. _____
5. _____

☐ **3x3**

How I want to **show up** today in one word:
_____

How I want to **feel** today in one word:
_____

If I only **got one thing done today,** it must be:
_____

5 AM	
6 AM	
7 AM	
8 AM	
9 AM	
10 AM	
11 AM	
12 PM	
1 PM	
2 PM	
3 PM	
4 PM	
5 PM	
6 PM	
7 PM	
8 PM	
9 PM	

DAILY SECTION

MM _____ DD _____ YR _____ QQ _____

REFLECT & RESET™ (PM)

I drank _____ ounces of water.   I moved my body for _____ minutes.

Something I realized or a lesson I learned today: _____

_____

Something that happened today that I really appreciated: _____

_____

☐ Shut off all electronics 30 minutes before bed.

Accomplishments:

_____

_____

_____

_____

_____

Plans for Tomorrow:

_____

_____

_____

_____

_____

Notes

_____

_____

DAILY SECTION

PREPARE & PLAN™ (AM)

Five Things I'm Grateful for Today...

1. _____
2. _____
3. _____
4. _____
5. _____

☐ **3x3**

How I want to **show up** today in one word:

_____

How I want to **feel** today in one word:

_____

If I only **got one thing done today,** it must be:

_____

5 AM	
6 AM	
7 AM	
8 AM	
9 AM	
10 AM	
11 AM	
12 PM	
1 PM	
2 PM	
3 PM	
4 PM	
5 PM	
6 PM	
7 PM	
8 PM	
9 PM	

DAILY SECTION

REFLECT & RESET™ (PM)

I drank _____ ounces of water.   I moved my body for _____ minutes.

Something I realized or a lesson I learned today: _____
_____

Something that happened today that I really appreciated: _____
_____

☐ Shut off all electronics 30 minutes before bed.

Accomplishments:

_____
_____
_____
_____
_____

Plans for Tomorrow:

_____
_____
_____
_____

Notes

_____
_____

DAILY SECTION

MM _____ DD _____ YR _____ QQ _____

PREPARE & PLAN™ (AM)

Five Things I'm Grateful for Today...

1. _____
2. _____
3. _____
4. _____
5. _____

☐ 3x3

How I want to **show up** today in one word:

_____

How I want to **feel** today in one word:

_____

If I only **got one thing done today,** it must be:

_____

5 AM
6 AM
7 AM
8 AM
9 AM
10 AM
11 AM
12 PM
1 PM
2 PM
3 PM
4 PM
5 PM
6 PM
7 PM
8 PM
9 PM

DAILY SECTION

REFLECT & RESET™ (PM)

I drank _____ ounces of water. I moved my body for _____ minutes.

Something I realized or a lesson I learned today: _____
_____

Something that happened today that I really appreciated: _____
_____

☐ Shut off all electronics 30 minutes before bed.

Accomplishments:

_____
_____
_____
_____
_____

Plans for Tomorrow:

_____
_____
_____
_____
_____

Notes

_____
_____

Step 1. Capture and Collect any task or idea that's on your mind.

Simply transfer these items out of your head and onto the page. This is especially important as you consider your Monthly Goals and KPIs. What do you need to do this week to be successful?

CAPTURE **&** **COLLECT**

"Your financial reports—rich with metrics and KPIs—make up the Profit Playbook guiding your overall winning strategy."

— Candy Valentino

WEEK 4

Step 2. Categorize your tasks or ideas.

Group like tasks or ideas together to create easier visualization and execution.

CATEGORIZE

Category:	Category:	Category:
_____	_____	_____
_____	_____	_____
_____	_____	_____
_____	_____	_____
_____	_____	_____
_____	_____	_____

Category:	Category:	Category:
_____	_____	_____
_____	_____	_____
_____	_____	_____
_____	_____	_____
_____	_____	_____

Step 3. DEA: Delegate, Eliminate, and Automate.

- **Delegate:** Delegate any item possible to your team.
- **Eliminate:** Strikethrough any item that doesn't meet Pareto's Principle: 20% of your action creates 80% of your results.
- **Automate:** Write an "A" next to any items that you can use a system to automate.

DAILY SECTION

PREPARE & PLAN™ (AM)

Five Things I'm Grateful for Today...

1. _____
2. _____
3. _____
4. _____
5. _____

☐ **3x3**

How I want to **show up** today in one word:
_____

How I want to **feel** today in one word:
_____

If I only **got one thing done today,** it must be:
_____

5 AM	
6 AM	
7 AM	
8 AM	
9 AM	
10 AM	
11 AM	
12 PM	
1 PM	
2 PM	
3 PM	
4 PM	
5 PM	
6 PM	
7 PM	
8 PM	
9 PM	

DAILY SECTION

REFLECT & RESET™ (PM)

I drank _____ ounces of water.   I moved my body for _____ minutes.

Something I realized or a lesson I learned today: _____
_____

Something that happened today that I really appreciated: _____
_____

☐ Shut off all electronics 30 minutes before bed.

Accomplishments:

_____
_____
_____
_____
_____

Plans for Tomorrow:

_____
_____
_____
_____
_____

Notes

_____
_____

DAILY SECTION

MM _____ DD _____ YR _____ QQ _____

PREPARE & PLAN™ (AM)

Five Things I'm Grateful for Today...

1. _____
2. _____
3. _____
4. _____
5. _____

☐ **3x3**

How I want to **show up** today in one word:
_____

How I want to **feel** today in one word:
_____

If I only **got one thing done today,** it must be:
_____

5 AM	
6 AM	
7 AM	
8 AM	
9 AM	
10 AM	
11 AM	
12 PM	
1 PM	
2 PM	
3 PM	
4 PM	
5 PM	
6 PM	
7 PM	
8 PM	
9 PM	

DAILY SECTION

_____

REFLECT & RESET™ (PM)

💧 I drank _____ ounces of water.   🏋 I moved my body for _____ minutes.

Something I realized or a lesson I learned today: _____

_____

Something that happened today that I really appreciated: _____

_____

☐ Shut off all electronics 30 minutes before bed.

Accomplishments:

_____
_____
_____
_____
_____

Plans for Tomorrow:

_____
_____
_____
_____
_____

Notes

_____
_____

DAILY SECTION

MM _____ DD _____ YR _____ QQ _____

PREPARE & PLAN™ (AM)

Five Things I'm Grateful for Today...

1. _____
2. _____
3. _____
4. _____
5. _____

☐ 3x3

How I want to **show up** today in one word:
_____

How I want to **feel** today in one word:
_____

If I only **got one thing done today,** it must be:
_____

5 AM	
6 AM	
7 AM	
8 AM	
9 AM	
10 AM	
11 AM	
12 PM	
1 PM	
2 PM	
3 PM	
4 PM	
5 PM	
6 PM	
7 PM	
8 PM	
9 PM	

DAILY SECTION

REFLECT & RESET™ (PM)

💧 I drank _____ ounces of water.   🏋 I moved my body for _____ minutes.

Something I realized or a lesson I learned today: _____

_____

Something that happened today that I really appreciated: _____

_____

☐ Shut off all electronics 30 minutes before bed.

Accomplishments:

_____

_____

_____

_____

Plans for Tomorrow:

_____

_____

_____

_____

_____

Notes

_____

_____

DAILY SECTION

PREPARE & PLAN™ (AM)

Five Things I'm Grateful for Today...

1. _____
2. _____
3. _____
4. _____
5. _____

☐ **3x3**

How I want to **show up** today in one word:
_____

How I want to **feel** today in one word:
_____

If I only **got one thing done today,** it must be:
_____

5 AM	
6 AM	
7 AM	
8 AM	
9 AM	
10 AM	
11 AM	
12 PM	
1 PM	
2 PM	
3 PM	
4 PM	
5 PM	
6 PM	
7 PM	
8 PM	
9 PM	

DAILY SECTION

REFLECT & RESET™ (PM)

💧 I drank _____ ounces of water. 🏋 I moved my body for _____ minutes.

Something I realized or a lesson I learned today: _____

_____

Something that happened today that I really appreciated: _____

_____

☐ Shut off all electronics 30 minutes before bed.

Accomplishments:

_____

_____

_____

_____

_____

Plans for Tomorrow:

_____

_____

_____

_____

Notes

_____

_____

DAILY SECTION

MM _____ DD _____ YR _____ QQ _____

_____

PREPARE & PLAN™ (AM)

Five Things I'm Grateful for Today...

1. _____
2. _____
3. _____
4. _____
5. _____

☐ **3x3**

How I want to **show up** today in one word:
_____

How I want to **feel** today in one word:
_____

If I only **got one thing done today,** it must be:
_____

5 AM	
6 AM	
7 AM	
8 AM	
9 AM	
10 AM	
11 AM	
12 PM	
1 PM	
2 PM	
3 PM	
4 PM	
5 PM	
6 PM	
7 PM	
8 PM	
9 PM	

DAILY SECTION

_____

REFLECT & RESET™ (PM)

I drank _____ ounces of water.   I moved my body for _____ minutes.

Something I realized or a lesson I learned today: _____

_____

Something that happened today that I really appreciated: _____

_____

☐ Shut off all electronics 30 minutes before bed.

Accomplishments:

_____
_____
_____
_____
_____

Plans for Tomorrow:

_____
_____
_____
_____
_____

Notes

_____
_____

QUARTERLY GOAL REVIEW

Step 1. Reflect on your progress.

**Evaluate how closely you've met your quarterly goal.
Did you achieve it?**

_____

_____

_____

**If not, what percentage of the goal was accomplished?
Use that metric to write your goal.**

I met _____ % of my goal to increase my _____ from _____ to _____

How did your financial performance change over the quarter?

_____

_____

_____

_____

Step 2. Assess your strategies.

This review will help you close the current quarter with a clear understanding of your achievements and areas for improvement, setting a solid foundation for the next quarter's goals and strategies.

Which strategies and actions contributed most to your progress?

Identify what worked well and what didn't:

WORKED	DIDN'T WORK

QUARTERLY GOAL REVIEW

MM _____ DD _____ YR _____ QQ _____

Step 3. Assess your progress.

Key Learnings:
Document the most valuable insights you've gained during this quarter.

VALUABLE INSIGHTS

What lessons can you apply going forward?

_____

_____

Challenges Encountered:
Discuss any significant obstacles you faced and how you addressed them. Are there any ongoing issues that need attention?

_____

_____

Next Quarter Planning:
Based on this quarter's performance and insights, set preliminary goals for the next quarter. Were there any goals from this quarter that can be completed next quarter?

_____

_____

Personal Development:
Reflect on your personal growth as a leader and entrepreneur. How have you evolved, and what areas do you want to develop next quarter?

_____

_____

Action Steps for Improvement:
Outline specific actions you will take to address challenges and leverage opportunities in the next quarter.

CONGRATULATIONS!

Congrats on completing your next quarter toward your wealthiest year yet!

It's easy to start something, but hard to finish. By completing this planner you are already on your way to becoming part of the **9%**.

Remember, building with intention and planning your success is a powerful and necessary step toward achieving your goals. We have only just begun. Here are your next steps to keep the momentum going!

Order Your Next 9% Edge Quarterly Planner.

Place your purchase one week prior to the close of the quarter so you stay on track with those goals! Go here to place your order ***www.9PercentPlanner.com***

Prepare and Plan for Your Next Quarter.

As you approach the beginning of the next quarter, evaluate your goals and achievements. What successes can you stack on as you move into the next quarter. Business industries, markets, and revenue can change rapidly. Do you need to adjust, redirect, or change your goals – and therefore your strategy – for the next quarter?

Create Your Long-Term Vision.

While this planner is designed for quarterly use, it's also beneficial to conduct a comprehensive review of your business annually. This will help you identify long-term trends, build your revenue roadmap, plan your profit, celebrate significant milestones, and optimize for future growth.

Be a Life-Long Student.

All of the most successful people I know are life-long learners. Every week we drop new episodes of *The Candy Valentino Show* to help you grow your knowledge, and we share proven business and financial principles to expand your net worth. Scan the QR code to listen!

If you want support in your business and financial growth, head over to ***www.candyvalentino.com*** and learn more about Founders Organization and our Preferred Pro Partners.

Remember, you're worthy and capable of realizing your dreams and creating the life and business you want. Stay focused, and keep going. I'm cheering you on and can't wait to see you join me in the 9%.

ALSO FROM
CANDY
VALENTINO

WALL STREET JOURNAL BESTSELLING AUTHOR
CANDY VALENTINO

THE
9%
EDGE

THE LIFE-CHANGING SECRETS TO CREATE MORE REVENUE FOR YOUR BUSINESS AND MORE FREEDOM FOR YOURSELF

The 9% Edge • ISBN: 978-1-394-15232-2

WILEY